MW01275495

BABIES WITH RABIES
AN ABC SURVIVAL GUIDE

by L. A. Cunningham & David Molinero

ISBN 978-1-7779926-0-6

A is for always ...
ALWAYS be aware.
This book is your guide
to help you prepare.

B is for babies!
What this guide is about.
If a wild baby approaches,
try not to freak out.

C is for calm.
Keep a level head.
Just remember this training,
because you're no use dead.

D is for drool dripping from their chin.
And those pointed daggers in their menacing grin.

E is for eyes,
fevered and bright.
Sizing you up
to ruin your night.

hostility

force   Cuteness

speed   empathy

Demon haircut

Sharp baby nails
for clawing

fevered eyes
and acute vision

Pointed dagger-like
teeth for tearing
and biting

Drool indicates
RABID
CONDITION!!

small legs
for scuttling
and agility

Absorbent diapers

F is for facts.
First, some basics to know.
Because the feral baby
is a formidable foe.

G is for gangs.
They may travel in packs.
Be sure to watch your front
but don't forget your back.

H is for help.
Don't face them alone.
Especially outnumbered,
it's too hard on your own.

I is for incisors
looking to chew.
Be thankful you have ten fingers,
'cause you may lose a few.

J is for your jugular,
ripped clean from your throat.
A fatal attack,
so make sure you take note.

K is for Kevlar–
and not just a vest.
Head-to-toe coverage
will protect you the best.

L is for a light
to shine in their face.
When they're temporarily blinded,
get out of that place!

M is for montage.
You'll need to train.
You must strengthen your body,
as WELL as your brain.

N is for ninjutsu.

Sign up for a class.
You might think you don't need it,
but it could save your ass.

O is for ornery
but distractible little things.
Make sure you're armed
with lots of teething rings.

P is for painkillers
for them AND for you.
Need something stronger?
Tranquillizers work, too.

Q is for quiet.
Be still as a tree.
The babies can't kill
what the babies can't see.

R is for rabies.
Of COURSE it's for rabies!
Your most imminent threat
is BABIES WITH RABIES!

S is for shots.
Make sure you're up-to-date.
Needles are scary,
but there is a worse fate.

T is for teeth
that'll haunt your dreams.
Long after the battle,
you'll still hear the screams.

U is for

UUUUURRRRRGGGHHHHHH!

V is for victory,
in which there is none.
You made it through the day,
but the war is not won.

W is for weary.
It's an endless fight
against droves of babies
with a penchant to bite.

X is for-you know what?
Who cares about X!
Want fewer feral babies?
Two words: protected sex!

So **Y** is for "You're welcome for saving your skin."
With this guide and some luck,
the babies won't* win.

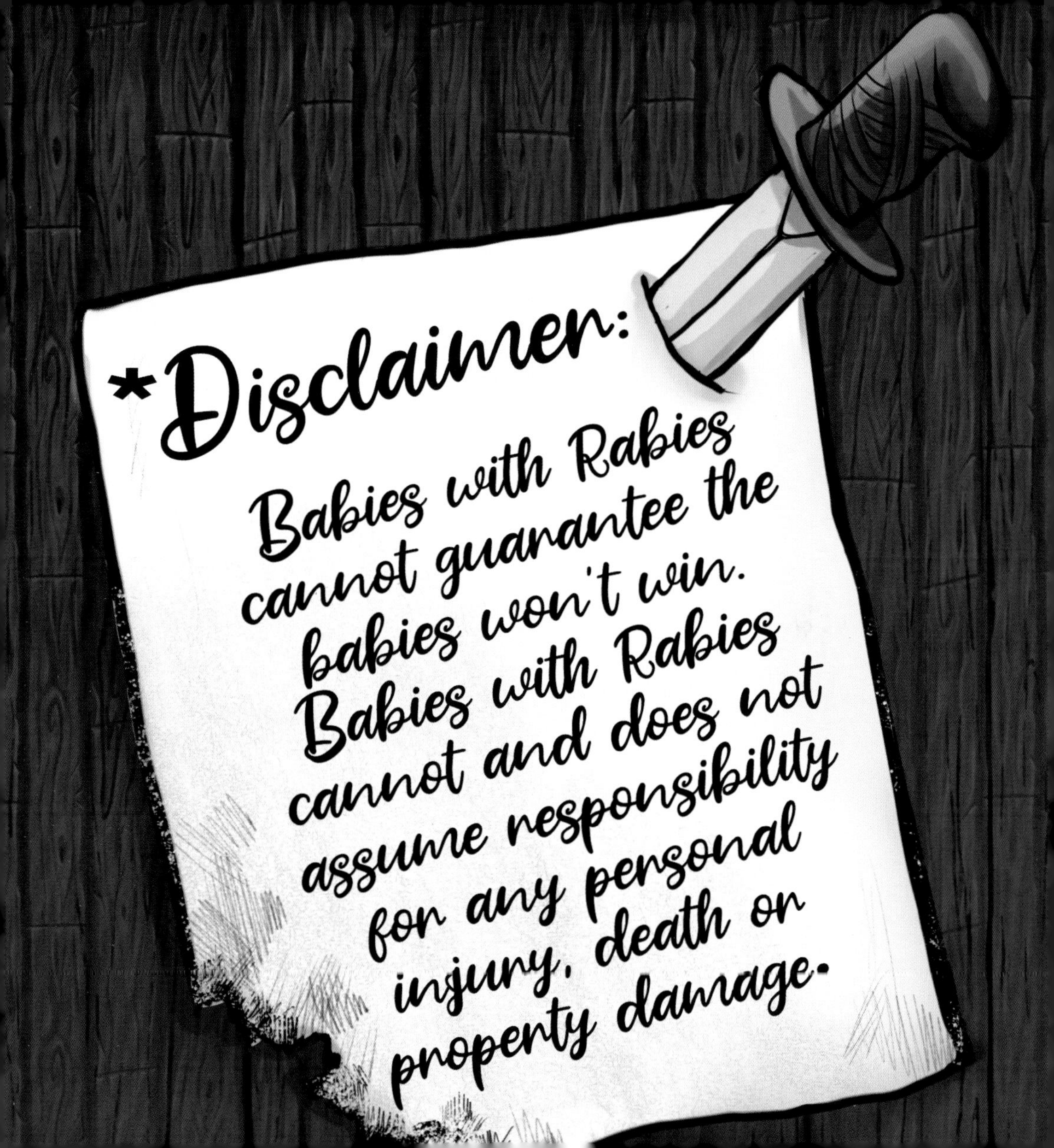
*Disclaimer:
Babies with Rabies
cannot guarantee the
babies won't win.
Babies with Rabies
cannot and does not
assume responsibility
for any personal
injury, death or
property damage.

And finally Z:
for the zero chances you can take.
When it comes to rabid babies,
too many lives are at stake.

Thanks to my family for supporting me and helping me find and make the time to complete this book. Thanks to Paul and Sarah for your brainstorming and editing services and for cheering me on. And a special thanks to my daughter for being my toothy, feral inspiration.

About Author:

L. A. Cunningham is an author and comic book creator with a dark and twisty sense of humour that pairs nicely with her dark and twisty writing. She and her spouse have two small human children and one larger canine child, all of whom enjoy eating food off the floor and watching squirrels out the window.